H K
HIS LIFE AND LOCOMOTIVES
Kenneth Allan Bullock

The Heywood Society
Plateway Press

ISBN 0 9511108 9 6

AUTHOR'S NOTE

Having inherited my father's passion for steam engines but not, alas, his ingenuity, I feel it is my humble duty to record in this book some of his remarkable achievements not least of which was the design, construction and re-construction of no less than seventeen 10¼in. gauge steam locomotives during the depression years of the 1930s. Most of his locomotives still survive today, a fair percentage of which are still operating.

My thanks must go to John Hall-Craggs and Brian Hollingsworth for their great help and encouragement, and to Freda Ridgett for her help with the typing; also to my son Keith for his diagrams and moral support. I must also acknowledge the debt I owe to John Hall-Craggs and Brian Hollingsworth, Matthew Kerr, James Nutty and Simon Townsend for generously lending from their private collections many precious photographs for the book.

Kenneth Allan Bullock takes charge of his father's first 10¼in gauge locomotive, on the last day of operation of the Meadow End Rly, Brockenhurst, Hants, 1966. His son Keith stands on the left.

Edited and designed by Brian Hollingsworth.

Printed by Snowdonia Press, Porthmadog, Gwynedd.

Published by Plateway Press, 13 Church Rd, Croydon, Surrey, CR0 1SG on behalf of The Heywood Society.

Cover: 4-6-2 No.2005 KING GEORGE VI on the Stonecot Hill Railway.

Frontispiece: 4-6-2 No. 2005 SILVER JUBILEE, designed and built by H.C.S. Bullock, brings a happy trainload into the station on the long-vanished 10¼in. gauge railway at Bramber Castle.

H.C.S. Bullock at Fox Hill motive power depot in 1937, engaged in preparing one of his magnificent locomotives for the road.

CONTENTS

CHAPTER I — PEACE and WAR

My father's interest in steam locomotives became apparent when he was old enough to bite the shape of an engine out of his bread and butter! He was born in 1889 and spent much of his childhood with his two brothers in the Wiltshire village of Box, where his father was a signalman on the Great Western Railway at Box station, working in the famous BOX SIGNAL BOX. Like most young lads, the brothers were not beyond getting up to a certain amount of mischief and I recall the times my father spent telling us of some of the pranks which did not always work out the way they were planned.

One such occasion happened after the Council had left a wooden tar barrel at the top of the hill in the village in readiness for some road repairs. Opposite lived a rather grumpy local dignitary. The boys, therefore, decided to leave this gentleman the tar barrel outside the front door as a present. Unfortunately, en route to its destination, the barrel ran out of control and plunged down the hill towards the Northy Arms Hotel, on the Bath Road, finally smashing itself against a stone wall halfway down the hill. Evidence of the incident could still be seen as late as 1975!!

After spending a short time as a cleaner at the G.W.R. Swindon works, Father moved into lodgings at Pilning, Gloucestershire, and obtained work in the pumping station at Speedwell Colliery. He soon showed an ability in drawing and produced some fine sketches of the saddle-tank locomotive, the winding gear and the boiler house at the colliery. In February 1909, Father enrolled in the 4th Gloucester Regiment, transferring to the Royal Flying Corps in June 1912. He was then posted to Farnborough, Hants, with No.2 Squadron, moving to Montrose, Scotland, in February 1913.

During these early pioneering days of the R.F.C., many activities of an inventive and experimental nature were taking place, not least of which was a continuous effort to increase the distance range of the aeroplane. It was during this development period that a 'Length of Flight Time' record was achieved. Quoting from 'WAR IN THE AIR' by Rayleigh, vol.I "In the front seat of a B.E. machine, 1st class Air Mechanic H.C.S.Bullock fitted a petrol tank of his own design estimated to give at least eight hours fuel for the 70hp Renault engine. On 22nd November 1913, Captain Longcroft took off in this aircraft and flew from Montrose to Portsmouth, circling inland finally landing at Farnborough in 7hours 20min non-stop". My father built a fine model of the aircraft concerned.

At the outbreak of World War I No.2 Squadron were sent to France and soon saw action. Whilst my father was flying low over enemy lines as Observer to this same Captain Longcroft their aircraft came under some heavy rifle fire and was subsequently forced to land through loss of oil pressure. It was soon discovered that a bullet had damaged a feed pipe causing serious loss of oil. By using strips torn from his shirt sleeve, Father was able to effect a temporary repair and restart the engine, taking off virtually in sight of a German patrol which had been sent to capture them. My father got married in Montrose during 1915. His bride was a girl from Montrose called

Helen Alexander. They had more time together than most young newly-married couples in those terrible days because my father received shrapnel wounds on Christmas Day and he was then sent home for six months' sick leave. After this he returned to France for a further tour of duty, this time with No. 8 Squadron.

At this time my father was involved with the problems of night flying, which at that time involved so many casulties without any compensating success that the authorities had to consider prohibiting it altogether. My father played an important part in the development of a device or apparatus — it is not clear exactly what this was — which would assist pilots in this hazardous operation. His work played a significant part in Lieutenant Robinson's success in bringing down the Zeppelin L22 at 2.45am on 3rd of September 1916.

My father was eventually posted home in 1917 and he served at the Central Flying School, the Aerial Gunnery Schools at Hythe and Loch Doon and the Experimental Station at Orfordness. While at Hythe, father's efforts in an experimental capacity to bring about a successful launching of an aerial torpedo was also noted. During his time at Orfordness my father was sent to Felixtowe to re-organize the workshops on the coast which catered for the repair and maintenance of small naval craft.

Of the 21 vessels which comprised the normal strength of the establishment only a handful were seaworthy when we arrived. By setting an example — in borrowed overalls! — and personally involving himself he was able to bring the unit up to full strength in a comparatively short time. There is a report of my father pointing out to higher authority that an expensive and elaborate scheme to drain some land to the north of the base at Montrose was a non-starter for various reasons, not least of which was the effect of the tidal basin at Montrose on the level of the coastal waters. At times they were above the level of the airstrip! Being a junior officer his technical advice fell on deaf years among the hierarchy — but in the end after much cost and wasted time the scheme had to be abandoned for the reasons my father put in his report.

My father left the service in 1919 after a distinguished career with the rank of captain. He received the M.B.E. in January 1918, followed by a Mention in Despatches in March. He had been awarded the Military Medal in January 1916 for his exploit with Captain Longcroft and in the connection it must be said that he was never without a sense of humour. On the occasion that he summoned to Buckingham Palace to receive his decoration, the overnight train from Scotland was so late that it left no time for him to have a shave. When at the Investiture ceremony, King George V asked him where he had served last. My father thought His Majesty had said "where did you shave last" to which the reply was "Scotland Sir" The King looked bewildered, probably as the Military Medal was awarded for gallantry in the field!

After leaving the service, my father moved south to join his two brothers at Palmerston Road, Boscombe, Hampshire, where by 1920 they had built a light car named 'The Palmerston'. It was spoken of as 'a machine of simple and pleasing appearance" and its builder claimed it to be the first in the light car field. It was described in both 'Light Car and Cyclecar' (26 June, 1920) and in the 'Autocar' (13 November, 1920).

The cost of the baby car was £250 and it was a two-seater with a 'dickie' seat. It was driven by a 680cc. Coventry 'Victor' water-cooled engine and could

The 5-6 h.p. Palmerston chassis has a miniature horizontally opposed water–cooled engine.

return 55 miles to the gallon. An interesting feature was a transmission brake. The illustrations below and on the previous page were supplied by the Library of the Montagu Motor Museum, Beaulieu, Hants.

In 1921 a slightly enlarged and rather more powerful model was introduced, with a 1018cc. engine. Both models were still available in 1922, when they were included in the Autocar's 'Illustrated Review of 1922 Models'. However, only a small number of the cars was produced — none of which have survived — and it must be said that father's sojourn in the car Manufacturing business was not a complete success. But a move to Farnborough was in the offing.

Three-quarter front view of the Palmerston.

The bodywork lines of the Palmerston light car are simple and give the machine a pleasing appearance.

Key to MAP on opposite page of FARNBOROUGH AREA

1. Fowler Road, Cove
2. 'The Olives', Prospect Avenue
3. Course of Fox Hill Miniature Railway
4. Site of Ratcliffe's Farm
5. The Fox Inn, Hawley
6. Course of Surrey Border and Camberley Railway

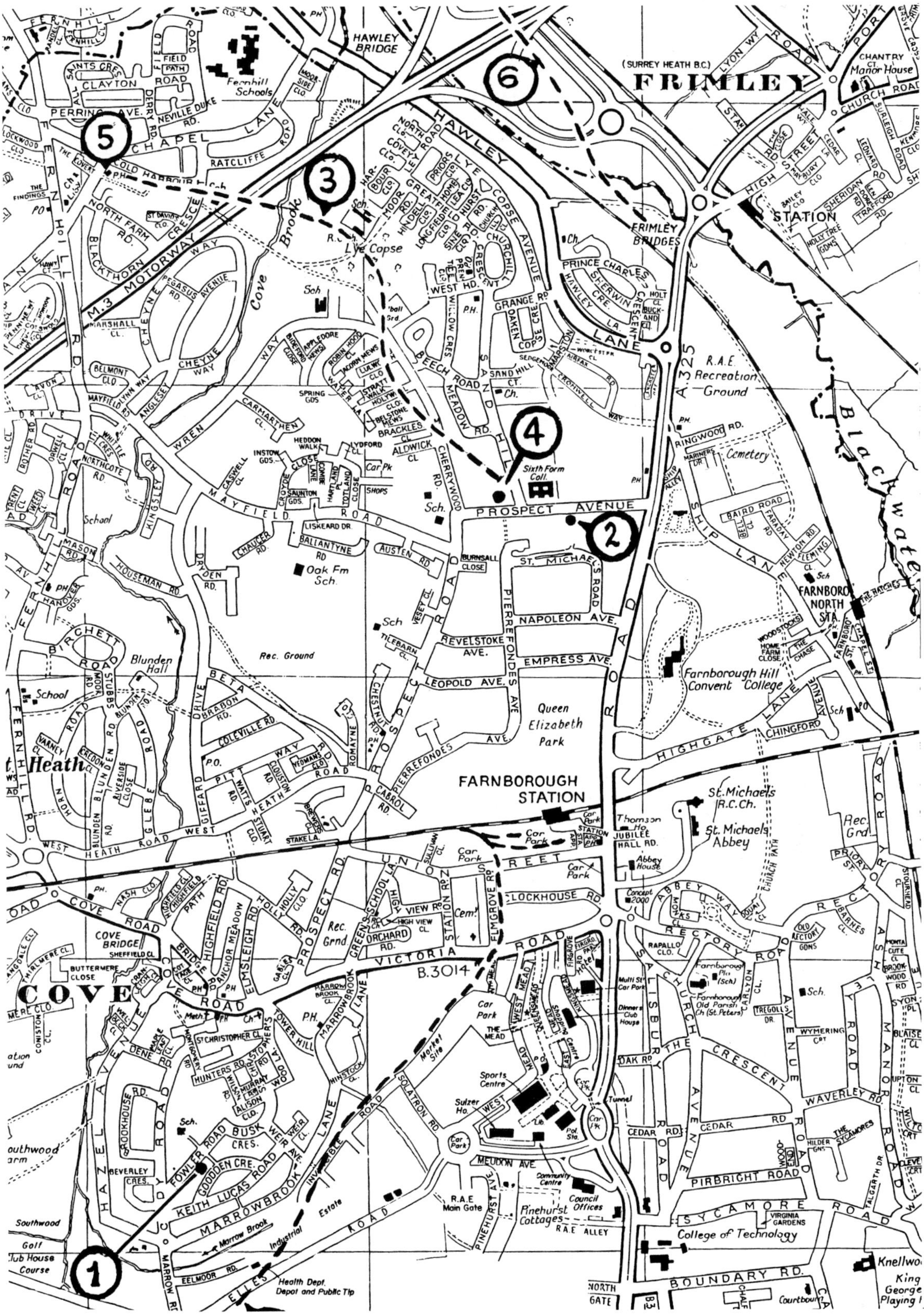
1
2
3
4
5
6
FRIMLEY
(SURREY HEATH B.C.)
HAWLEY BRIDGE
Fernhill Schools
CLAYTON ROAD
PERRING AVE.
CHAPEL LANE
RATCLIFFE ROAD
NEVILLE DUKE RD.
COLD HARBOUR LA.
NORTH FARM RD.
BLACKTHORN CRESC.
M.3 MOTORWAY
Cove Brook
Lye Copse
HAWLEY LANE
COPSE AVENUE
CHURCHILL CRESCENT
PRINCE CHARLES CRES.
FRIMLEY BRIDGES
HIGH STREET
STATION
CHANTRY CT.
Manor House
CHURCH ROAD
PORTSMOUTH ROAD
LYON WY
R.A.E. Recreation Ground
A.325
Blackwater
RINGWOOD RD.
Cemetery
BAIRD ROAD
SHIP LANE
FARNBORO' NORTH STA.
Farnborough Hill Convent College
HIGHGATE LANE
CHINGFORD AVENUE
CHEYNE WAY
PEGASUS AVENUE
MARSHALL CL.
BELMONT CLO.
MAYFIELD RD
WREN WAY
CARMARTHEN CL.
BEECH ROAD
SAND HILL
Sixth Form Coll.
PROSPECT AVENUE
ST. MICHAEL'S ROAD
NAPOLEON AVE.
EMPRESS AVE.
REVELSTOKE AVE.
LEOPOLD AVE.
PIERREFONDES AVE
Queen Elizabeth Park
MAYFIELD ROAD
Oak Fm Sch.
Rec. Ground
PROSPECT ROAD
FERNHILL ROAD
BIRCHETT ROAD
Blunden Hall
School
Heath
WEST HEATH ROAD
FARNBOROUGH STATION
St. Michaels R.C.Ch.
St. Michaels Abbey
JUBILEE HALL RD.
UNION STREET
CLOCKHOUSE RD
ABBEY WAY
RECTORY ROAD
Rec. Grd
COVE ROAD
COVE BRIDGE
COVE
VICTORIA ROAD
B.3014
Rec. Grnd
Cem.
Car Park
Market Site
Sports Centre
Sulzer Ho.
Council Offices
Community Centre
Pinehurst Cottages
R.A.E. Main Gate
MEUDON AVE
PINEHURST AVE
SALISBURY ROAD
CHURCH AVENUE
THE CRESCENT
CEDAR RD
WAVERLEY RD.
PIRBRIGHT ROAD
SYCAMORE ROAD
College of Technology
BOUNDARY RD.
Knellwood
King George Playing
HAZEL AVENUE
FOWLER ROAD
BUSK CRES.
GOODDEN CRE.
KEITH LUCAS ROAD
MARROWBROOK LANE
Marrow Brook
Industrial Estate
INVINCIBLE ROAD
SOLATRON ROAD
EELMOOR RD.
ELLES ROAD
Health Dept. Depot and Public Tip
Southwood Golf Club House Course
NORTH GATE
R.A.E. ALLEY

5in.gauge 4-6-0 No.6000 KING GEORGE V built at Fowler Road in 1927.

CHAPTER II — LOCOMOTIVE CONSTRUCTION BEGINS

In 1923 my father joined the Air Ministry and was sent from London to work in the Design Department at the Royal Aircraft Establishment, Farnborough. Here he was given staff quarters in Fowler Road, Cove. This was his chance to begin locomotive building and soon the first of his locomotives appeared. It was a 2-4-2 wooden toy with handles attached to the cab sides to assist the author — then aged fifteen months — in the art of walking! Two 4-6-0 locomotives followed, one each for my brother and me, built to the three-inch gauge. They were fired by methylated spirit in a tray under the boiler, which was made from a cocoa tin. Serious construction began in 1924 and over the next few years seven 5in. gauge engines were built :-

4-2-2	DUKE OF CONNAUGHT	G.W.R. 'Achilles' class
0-4-0T		Free-lance design
4-2-2	BLACK PRINCE	Rebuilt 'Achilles' class
4-4-0	BULLDOG	G.W.R 'Bulldog' class
4-6-0	PENDENNIS CASTLE	G.W.R. 'Castle' class
4-6-0	KING GEORGE V	G.W.R. 'King' class
4-6-2	LADY HAZEL JUNE	G.W.R. style

Above, left: 5in.gauge GWR-style 0-4-0T, Ken Bullock too interested in driving to look at the camera.
Above, right: GWR 'Achilles' class 4-2-2 BLACK PRINCE hauls a load of young Bullocks away from the platform.

LADY HAZEL JUNE (shown above, before completion) was intended as a modernised version of the G.W.R. 4-6-2 THE GREAT BEAR. She was the prototype for my father's subsequent larger locomotives. Both DUKE of CONNAUGHT, PENDENNIS CASTLE (seen below) and KING GEORGE V gained major awards at Model Engineer Exhibitions, the former winning the Bronze Medal in 1927 and the latter the Silver in 1928. All the locomotives together with a number of steam-driven feed pumps which my father had made and patented, were sold to Captain Holder of 'Keeping', Bucklers Hard, Beaulieu, Hants. Holder who also placed an order for a 10¼ in. gauge 'pacific' to supplement his two 'atlantics', PETER PAN by Bassett-Lowke and JOHN TERENCE by Grimshaw, the Holders' mechanic before they moved to Hampshire.

5in. gauge locomotive PENDENNIS CASTLE. Awarded the Bronze Medal at the Model Engineer Exhibition in 1927.

Parts of No.1001 THE MONARCH at an early stage of construction, outside the workshop at Fowler Road, 1930.

No.1001 THE MONARCH awaits the boiler at Fowler Road, 1931.

No.1001 THE MONARCH as delivered to Captain Holder. Baker valve gear still present, sand dome not yet fitted.

No.1001 now AUDREY. as altered. Note Walschaerts valve gear and addition of sand dome, seen also below in close-up.

LAYOUT OF THE OLIVES, PROSPECT AVE. FARNBOROUGH

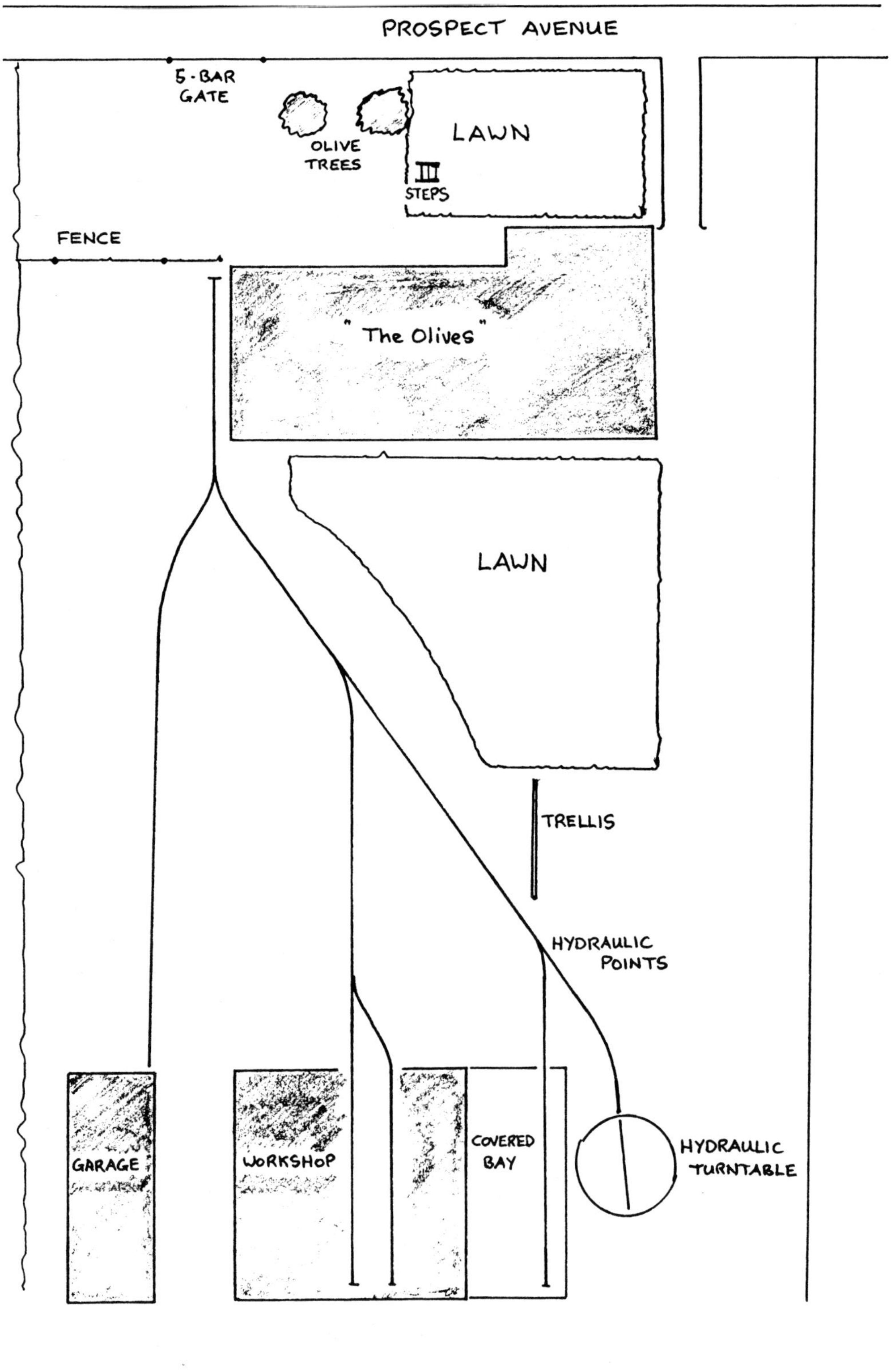

J.N. Maskelyne, editor of the magazine Model Engineer, drives AUDREY across the lawn at 'Keeping', 1935.

In 1932 THE MONARCH was completed, this being the first Bullock 10¼in. gauge locomotive. Once it had been delivered to Captain Holder, the ensuing weeks were devoted to dismantling the workshop at Fowler Road and moving everything to our new house 'The Olives' in Prospect Avenue, Farnborough. 'The Olives' was a spacious four-bedroomed dwelling jointly designed by Mr Hilder, the manager of a local firm of builders, and my father.

The drawing office, where my father was to spend most of his time was light and roomy and overlooked the copper beeches of Prospect woods. As can be seen on the plan the garden at the rear was 120ft in length and on the right hand side a large workshop was built with two tracks concreted into the floor at ground level. These led out to a set of points in the drive, providing a single track which curved towards the house and then ran parallel to the wall, terminating in line with the front of the building. A pair of heavy gates concealed the view from Prospect Avenue.

Looking back, I feel the days at Fowler Road were happier and more settled ones for my father, as he seemed to have more time to spend with us children. Indeed as the family increased so became the need for

The workshops at 'The Olives' where WESTERN QUEEN is awaiting her boiler, 1933.

a larger car than the 'drophead' Talbot with its 'dickie' seat, which had served as the family car. My father solved the accomodation problem by removing the original body and fitting a saloon type, which he made himself by laminating plywood and sealing it with fabric materials. His method of securing the front of the roof to the existing windscreen was to utilize the two vertical threaded stays and screw down wing nuts in concealed apertures.

However, on the road the wood soon began to squeak on the brass windscreen frame, so packing was placed between the two faces at each side. This packing usually consisted of halfpennies and sometimes even pennies!

It was not long before certain younger members of the family discovered this hidden treasure trove, which meant there were more frequent trips to the sweet shop than ever before.

Dad continued to replace the packing as often as it 'dropped out'. I would like to think that he knew all the time what really had happened to it! The journeys we made through the Forest to see Captain Holder always seemed an adventure in the old Talbot as there was at least a 12-mile gap between 'filling stations', but how reassuring when we passed an AA patrolman on his motor cycle and sidecar, receiving the customary salute when he saw the AA badge on the radiator.

4-6-2 No. THE EMPRESS was the next locomotive to be built and was as described on page 40. She took over twelve months to complete, being finished in 1933 and sold to Mr Cookson of Billingshurst, Sussex. As with No.1001 she was finished in G.W.R. green with a copper-top chimney. THE EMPRESS was taken away on a trailer towed behind a big black green Morris 18hp saloon.

Above: The workshops at 'The Olives', Prospect Avenue, with the famous 9½in, gauge London Brighton & South Coast Railway's Stroudley 0-4-2T RANMORE in for overhaul. Note the Bullock Citroen family car in its garage

Opposite, below: 4-6-2 No.1003 WESTERN QUEEN faces the open gate to Prospect Avenue from 'The Olives' in 1934, prior to transportation to Burnham-on-Sea.

No. 1002 THE EMPRESS tells the World she should have been really and truly Great Western.

CHAPTER III — FULL-TIME ENGINE BUILDER

After the completion of No.1002, my father resigned from the Royal Aircraft Establishment to concentrate on the design, construction and reconstruction of locomotives for the 10¼in. gauge. The single-wheeler from the Holders' earlier line at Pitmaston Moor (modelled on the Great Northern Railway's Stirling No.1 and built by Grimshaw before 1910) was at 'Keeping' about this time and was brought to Farnborough to be rebuilt. This included the replacement of the copper boiler by a larger steel one. This rebuilding took place alongside the third 'pacific' then under construction, No.1003 WESTERN QUEEN.

When both these jobs were completed in 1934, No.1003 and the 4-2-2 went to Mr Ballance of Burnham-on-Sea, Somerset. No.1003 was of similar dimensions to the other 4-6-2s but with two injectors and detail alterations to boiler fittings.

A second locomotive for Captain Holder, a 4-6-4T numbered 1004, to be named MARY, had reached a near state of completion towards the end of 1934. Alongside No.1004 in the workshop was the old Bassett-Lowke 4-4-2 PETER PAN of Wembley Exhibition fame, which was undergoing a rebuild including regauging from 9½in. gauge to 10¼in. It had come up from 'Keeping' during the summer.

My Father's policy of using standard parts for his locomotives wherever possible, i.e. wheel and cylinder castings, axle-boxes and horn blocks etc., enabled him to cut down on the labour and expense of having to produce several different patterns and drawings for the chassis. In fact, the engine parts of his locomotives were virtually identical up to No.1004.

4-2-2 Stirling No. 1 and WESTERN QUEEN stand awaiting custom on the Burnham-on-Sea Miniature Railway.

4-4-2 locomotive PETER PAN of Wembley Exhibition fame, overhauled by Bullock at Prospect Avenue, on Captain Holder's railway, 1935. Note the train of L.N.E.R. teak-built carriages.

4-6-4T No. 1004 MARY in the grounds of 'Keeping', 1934.

JOHN TERENCE in action on Captain Holder's Railway.

The six-coupled tank locomotive rebuilt by H.C.S. Bullock for Mr Burgoyne's 9½in. gauge. Spring Lanes Light Railway at Bracknell in 1935.

Nevertheless, things were getting somewhat hectic at Prospect Avenue during this period. An order from Mr Cookson for an additional locomotive had been placed, while the now rebuilt PETER PAN had been replaced by the other 4-4-2 JOHN TERENCE, also from Captain Holder. There was also a six-coupled 9½in. gauge tank engine from the Spring Lanes Light Railway at Bracknell, owned by Mr V.Burgoyne. All these jobs were dealt with at the same time.

First to emerge in the spring of 1935 was 4-6-2 No.2005 PRINCESS MARINA, The locomotive for Mr Cookson. It had slide-valve instead of piston-valve cylinders, of 5in. stroke by 3½in. bore and 14in. dia. driving wheels. This engine was heavier and with a working pressure of 140lbs/sq.in. was more powerful than any of the previous ones. It was the first of Bullock's second design. In addition to high- and low- pressure injectors, No.2005 had a feed pump fitted on the right-hand running plate.

As was normal practice with all the locomotives turned out, No.2005 was blocked up with the driving wheels well clear of the ground and run in at full working pressure for a day, alternating between forward and back gear. A partial application of the steam brake from time to time to stimulate load, would greatly increase the sound of the exhaust beat, so I was glad when my stint to look after the engine came round again, although Dad was never far away.

The name PRINCESS MARINA was changed to SILVER JUBILEE prior to leaving Prospect Avenue, to mark the celebrations of that year. In fact soon after arrival at Billingshurst Mr Cookson had the oil cups, clack boxes, hand-rails and other detail fittings removed and chromium plated. SILVER JUBILEE looked resplendent double-headed with THE EMPRESS on Mr Cookson's picturesque private line in West Sussex. Even before No.2005 had been completed, however, work was well under way on the next 4-6-2, No.2005 EDWARD VIII.

4-6-2 No.2005 SILVER JUBILEE in action on Mr Cookson's railway at Billinghurst, Sussex.

JOHN TERENCE had been satisfactorily steam-tested after its rebuild and duly returned to Captain Holder and, in addition the 9½in. gauge tank engine from Mr Burgoyne's line had been finished. Apart from a very diminutive orange-painted 0-4-2T in the workshop for valve setting, EDWARD VIII was then the sole occupant of the workshop.

The work-load at Prospect Avenue had been eased slightly by sending out the wheel and cylinder castings for machining to a light engineering works at North Camp, near Aldershot. This was owned by a Mr Panting, known locally as 'Digger'. My brother Charles and I were also involved, in keeping the workshop floor un-cluttered as well as such tasks as drilling pilot holes, de-burring axle-boxes after milling and turning and facing buffers on the centre lathe.

Another new arrival in the workshop was a North Eastern type 4-4-0 No.2015 sent in for rebuilding in the style of an LNER 'Super-Claud' 4-4-0, to be named WENDY. The number in this case was the number of the a protoype rather than my father's own number. It would not have fitted his ingenious scheme whereby the left-hand digit represented the number of the design, while the right hand ones represented the 'works number' of the locomotive in sequence. For example, No.1003 WESTERN QUEEN was the THIRD Bullock 10¼in. locomotive of the FIRST design.

Towards the end of the running season, my father made a trip to see the line at Burnham-on-Sea and discovered sand had been permitted to enter WESTERN QUEEN's lubricator. He made immediate arrangements for No.1003 and the little single-wheeler to be returned to Farnborough. This incident prompted my father to renew his efforts to acquire a suitable piece of land where he could have a quarter-mile or so of track for his own purposes. This was achieved late in 1935.

A nearby dairy farmer called 'Master' Bill Ratcliffe owned some pasture land, about half a mile from Prospect Avenue, which was known as 'Foxhills'. After some discussions, an arrangement was made between my father and Mr Ratcliffe to lease a strip of land on the lower part of the meadows to a point terminating in some woods which we knew as Lye Copse.

During the autumn of 1935, staff were employed to erect a shed about 30ft. long by 20ft. wide, at the closest point to the farm track. A water supply complete with drainage facilities was provided.

It was to this point that an immaculate WESTERN QUEEN, now in unlined black livery and with a squat cast-iron chimney, was delivered on a purpose-built two-wheeled trailer towed gingerly behind our big Citroen saloon car. Soon 12lb per yard rail began arriving from Messrs Francis Theakson and construction started of platforms for two roads.

The rail sections were dogged up on hardwood sleepers and after assembly loaded up to flat bogie wagons. Then they were propelled by WESTERN QUEEN to the work site and laid on to a prepared track bed. The bogie wagons were later completed to form some of the rolling stock for passenger haulage.

Top: The Great Northern single-wheeler No.1 from the Pitmaston Moor miniature railway, as rebuilt by Bullock, operating on the Farnborough Miniature Railway, 1936.

Centre: A 7¼in. gauge Great Central Railway 'Immingham' 4-6-0, overhauled at Fowler Road in 1931. The locomotive was subsequently advertised at £100.

Lower: 4-4-0 No.2015, based on the North Eastern 'R' (LNER D20) class, was also for rebuilding by Bullock.

A turntable was built at Prospect Avenue and set up in a prepared pit. It was experimentally operated by hydraulics, as was one set of points, but my father considered the hand-operated pump too slow in practice, so he abandoned the experiment. The turntable, which was to serve three roads, and the points were transported to the line in a very antiquated 3-ton Morris lorry which had been bought to transport equipment from the workshop. This was also used for collecting wheel castings from Wallis & Stevens, which were now going direct to Mr Cookson for machining and pressing on to the axles ready for bogie assembly at Fox Hill.

This work was very rewarding but a bit tedious, as each axle-box contained 15 rollers, and with eight axleboxes to pack with grease and load with bearings, plus eight covers with four spring washers and set screws for each coach. Assembly certainly made our fingers cold on those frosty winter mornings out on the platforms.

An all-steel bogie ballast wagon and a 60-gallon water tank wagon (a four wheeler) were built in the workshop and placed in service immediately. An all-weather saloon coach, designed by my father was also sent to the line. This coach was fitted with padded seats and finished in chocolate and cream livery. Two similar coaches were to follow, built by Baxter's Coach Works of Bagshot, Surrey.

Top: Demonstrating how locomotives were transported from the workshops, the Bullock family Citroen car arrives at the site of the F.H.M.R, trailing No. 1003 Western Queen.

Centre: Engineer's train about to depart from Fox Hill, carrying sections of pre-fabricated track. Note the ballast and tank wagons.

Right: With seven known WENDYs around at this time one cannot be too certain of the identity of this one, a 4-4-0 re-built by Bullock for the F.H.M.R.

Above and right: Two views of the boiler for 2006 under construction at Goodhands works.

CHAPTER IV — PARTNERSHIP

MR A.D.KINLOCH, a merchant banker of 20 Eaton Square, London, had been a frequent visitor to 'The Olives' for several weeks up to this period. It ultimately transpired that a more elaborate scheme, financed largely by Mr Kinloch, was then undertaken, with my father's role being that of 'Chief Mechanical Engineer & General Manager'.

Mr Ratcliffe agreed to the line being extended through the copse and into more meadow land to the Blackwater River and beyond to his boundary, which was about 100 yards west of the Fox Inn at Hawley. Mr Ratcliffe stipulated that the line be fully fenced and that a barrier be placed across it outside running hours between the copse and the Fox Hill side, to prevent cattle straying. This barrier was to figure in a dramatic turn of events later in the history of the railway.

Extra staff were employed to push on with the line through Lye Copse. Lighter 9lb per yd rail was now being used and a loop was established with spring-loaded points at each end. Several embankments had to be formed due to the boggy and undulating nature of the ground through the woods. It was not a very hospitable place to be during the winter and doubtless the men were glad to be out on the level ground again.

In due course the Blackwater River was bridged with rolled steel joists supported at each end by transoms, secured to wooden pilings driven into the bank. An emergency water tower was erected alongside the track on the Farnborough side of the river and a semi-rotary pump was mounted nearby to

Fox Hill — Above left to right: PRINCESS ELIZABETH; EDWARD VIII; HARVESTER; WESTERN QUEEN

Below: No. 3007 (driver — Ken Bullock), No. 3008 (driver — H.C.S. Bullock) heading a train of early coaches. Entry and exit must have been awkward, hence the opening roofs on later stock. EDWARD VIII and HARVESTER behind.

Mr A.D. Kinloch drives No.1003 WESTERN QUEEN on the Foxhill Miniature Railway in 1936. Note plain black livery and tender lettered 'L.N.E.R.' complete with coal rails.

supply the water. The track continued straight to a stiff pull up at 1 in 70 to Hawley Station buffer stops a few yards from the Fox Inn boundary. Three lines served the two platforms. The distance from Fox Hill to Hawley was just under one and a quarter miles. A reversing loop of 90ft.radius was added in 1937, so avoiding running round as well as tender-first running.

At Prospect Avenue No.2006 EDWARD VIII, now completed, was steamed to full pressure (140lbs per sq.in) to check the 'pop' safety valves, the first locomotive to be so fitted. There was also a five-element Swindon- type superheater as well as sanding gear. The whistle lay horizontally along the top of the Belpaire firebox and had a very distinctive tone. In most other respects No.2006 was similar to No.2005 but more powerful with cylinders of 4in. bore and 5in. stroke. Both locomotives had boilers by Goodhand Bros of Gillingham, Kent.

Two tank engines were under construction during the winter of 1935; they were 0-6-0Ts No.3007 and No.3008, with pannier and side tanks respectively. Both had inside cylinders 2½ x 4in. and 12in driving wheels. The working pressure was 125lb per sq.in. No.3008 was fitted with vacuum brakes and was the only Bullock locomotive so fitted. The rebuilt 4-4-0 WENDY was the second locomotive to arrive at Foxhill. She was renumbered No.2 and her presence enabled WESTERN QUEEN to have the luxury of an odd day off. WENDY was followed a week or two later by EDWARD VIII, the running shed having been considerably improved and made more secure to accomodate three locomotives.

Mr Kinloch and his close friend and confidant, Dr.Bernard, were frequent visitors to the railway, arriving fron London on Saturday and staying in Bagshot overnight, which would allow them another full day's driving on the Sunday. Mr Kinloch appeared to be uneasy whenever he drove EDWARD VIII, preferring the more docile WESTERN QUEEN. No.2006 had a tendency to prime and of course the 'pop' safety valves were inclined occasionally to startle the unsuspecting driver, to say the least!

No. 2005 PRINCESS MARINA at Prospect Avenue. She was renamed SILVER JUBILEE to mark the celebrations of 1935.

In due course the 0-6-0 pannier tank No.3007 was pushed outside the workshops at Prospect Avenue for her first steaming. Unfortunately, both injectors gave trouble with the result that eventually the fire had to be drawn. The problem, I seem to recall, had something to do with the water in the pannier tanks becoming too warm for the injectors to pick up without repeatedly ceasing to feed. However, the cause of the trouble was put right shortly afterwards and the locomotive was loaded on to the trailer and transported to Foxhill behind the old three-tonner.

In the new year my father made another complete change from the two tank locos by designing a replica A3 class L.N.E.R. 4-6-2. The engine took its number from its prototype No.2573 HARVESTER instead of following the system used for other locomotives. The leading particulars were:

Two piston-valve cylinders: 3.375in. bore x 4¾ in. stroke.
Working pressure: 140lb per sq.in.
Coupled wheels: 14½ in. diameter
Weight: 1ton 15cwt.

The whistle was as fitted to the full-size L.N.E.R. A4 class streamline pacifics.

Mr. Burgoyne having extended his line at Spring Lanes, Bracknell, was very keen to buy a Bullock 4-6-2, but with the order book full it would have been some considerable time before his needs were met. However, as Mr.Cookson was more than pleased with his slide-valve pacific No.2005, with its 14in. drivers and articulated coupling rods on his fairly restricted line, he agreed to sell THE EMPRESS back to my father but immediately placed an order for an identical engine to No.2005. Within a few days of her return to Farnborough, THE EMPRESS was loaded on to the trailer and taken to Foxhill. Here she was regularly steamed and used extensively over a period of about ten days, mostly being driven by Father. The locomotive was then re-gauged to 9½ in. in the Prospect Avenue workshops and delivered to Mr Burgoyne in time for the Easter holidays.

It had been hoped the Foxhill Miniature Railway would also be ready for Easter 1936 but it was not to be. The second tank engine No.3008 was now completed and delivered to the line without any difficulties. In addition the main water tower was now erected at the running sheds. A central-flow vertical boiler was placed next to the water tower and a steam-driven donkey-pump supplied the water to the tank. The also supplied a false draught for raising steam in the locomotives.

WESTERN QUEEN returns tender-first from Hawley to Fox Hill. Note the 20 m.p.h. limit sign — most such railways today do not aspire to such a speed even on the straight!

Actually this stationary boiler had rather a 'cranky' Ramsbottom type safety valve and more than once caused some faint-hearted members of the staff to scatter. It blew off at 75lb per sq.in. but on occasions the gauge would go beyond 100lbs if it were not watched carefully. The cure was to tap the valve lightly to start it, but it seems on one occasion a young painter working nearby had been instructed to keep his eye on the gauge and carry out the normal drill, but had momentarily forgotten to check. Whether he over-reacted may never be known, but it appears he discovered the pressure in the boiler had risen to 110lbs per sq.in. He then clouted the safety valve with such force that everything went up in the air, springs, weights, the lot ! — all lost in a cloud of steam. he fell into the turntable pit in his haste to get away.

There had been numerous runs with all the locomotives up and down the full length of the line to try and assess and arrive at some sort of timetable. Various combinations of motive power and rolling stock were tried. The rebuilt 4-2-2 which had been brought over from the workshops just after No.2006, was quite incapable of hauling more than one loaded coach up the 1 in 74/1 in 76 bank, since such a small percentage of its weight was available for adhension. The little single-driver was double-headed with WENDY from time to time when not used as station pilot.

'My' engine No.3007 and the 0-4-2T No.3008 performed well enough provided there was sufficient boiler pressure when we passed through the loop on the homeward journey. The difficulty was that, whereas the pacifics had an abundance of power to accelerate their trains away after the regulation slacks, my small tank engine needed time to 'blow-up'. She was usually rostered between two pacifics, one at Hawley and one at Fox Hill and this allowed me no time at Lye Copse for this pause for breath. Invariably a down train would be waiting to cross and I would have time only to slow down and exchange the token as authority to enter the single line section.

No. 2006 EDWARD VIII being turned on the Fox Hill turntable, 1937.

My father had a lucky escape on one occasion during these preliminary running days. Whilst driving the 0-4-2T with six empty bogies up from Hawley he approached Fox Hill station miles too fast. It will be remembered No.3008 had vacuum brakes and when applied these locked the wheels solid. This he did and the engine and train slid through the station towards the running shed and turntable, which fortunately was set for his road. He charged over the table, down the length of the engine house and straight through the end of the shed. Finally he emerged smiling with pieces of asbestos sheet all over the front of the engine. He commented to my brother and I, what good brakes they were!

One other near thing occurred to No.3008 whilst I was driving. To gain a road from the bay platform it was necessary simply to move up to the points, set the points, proceed till clear, reset, then continue. Having done all this but the last duty of re-setting, I made the grave error of leaving my engine in full forward gear instead of bringing the reversing lever back to mid-gear. Whilst walking back to the points the tanker started to move forward, there being a slight blow in the regulator. By the time I discovered the engine getting away it had already got a considerable lead on me. If ever I did a 100 yard sprint it must have been then, I leapt on to the buffers when the loco had gained a speed of about 15mph and brought it under control!

Earlier BLACK PRINCE, one of the 15in gauge Romney, Hythe & Dymchurch Railway's 4-6-2 locomotives, had parted company with its tender near Burmarsh Road whilst the driver had a hand on the regulator. As the engine surged forward the effect was toopen the lever even wider. It was some distance, I understood, before the locomotive tipped over. Captain Howey later in the year asked my father down to New Romney for a few days to convert the regulator action to an inward movement to open and vice versa to close.

No.2573 HARVESTER was not quite completed in time for the opening at Whitsun 1936 but there was adequate motive power 'on shed'. All the preparations for running a scheduled service had to be discarded as the public began to pile into the coaches as soon as they were emptied. The prototype saloon was very popular with the older folk.

The signal box was now open and this lent a touch of professionalism to the occasion. Sweets and ice-cream were on sale and the weather was perfect for the carnival-like proceedings. Some passengers bought several tickets at a time and it was altogether a very successful first opening day with everything running perfectly. Takings were about £75 from adult fares of one shilling (5p) and child fares of sixpence.

It was nightfall before the last locomotive was reversed into the running shed after the fire had been drawn and the glowing embers damped down on the track bed. HARVESTER had developed some lubrication problems with the cylinders during her initial trials but this was soon rectified and she too was placed in service, bringing the motive power up to a total of seven locomotives.

Above: A train of open carriages in use on the Fox Hill Miniature Railway.

Below: The famous closed 'Pullman Cars' of the F.H.M.R. solved the problem of getting a quart into a pint pot by having lifting roofs as well as opening doors, clearly shown in this picture.

Coaling up the tender before No. 1003 WESTERN QUEEN leaves Fox Hill for Hawley, 1937. Note that the 'Pullman' included as usual in the train is an unusually long one having three bays of seating instead of the normal two.

CHAPTER V — PROBLEMS, INCIDENTS and ACCIDENTS

Discussions had been taking place between my father and Mr Kinloch whilst HARVESTER was under construction, for a large 4-6-2 for the railway. The new locomotive required by Mr Kinloch was to be after the style of an L.M.S. 'Princess' class but no final decision had been made as regards the date of commencement of the project, up to the time that Mr Kinloch left for an extended holiday in Switzerland. All of Mr Kinloch's affairs were then left in the hands of his close friend and confidant Doctor Bernard.

A week or two after Mr Kinloch's departure, Dr. Bernard contacted my father to give him the go-ahead for the new engine. Accordingly steel for the frames was ordered and cut, axleboxes, hornblocks, brake gear, wheel and cylinder castings were bought from Wallis & Stevens and sent to Pantings for machining. Mr Cookson meanwhile had been pressing for a completion date for his engine which meant that my father was working a fifteen-hour day for weeks on end.

When Mr Kinloch returned from Europe to find work had advanced on the new 4-6-2, he immediately put a stop to it, claiming that Dr. Bernard had no right to sanction the commencement of the project. The frames and such of the chassis as had been assembled were removed to the far end of the workshop and covered with dust sheets, this representing a severe financial blow. Had the 4-6-2 been completed by my father it would have been numbered 4010, named PRINCESS MARGARET ROSE and finished in maroon livery.

In spite of all my father's efforts being concentrated on Mr Cookson's locomotive, it was still a bit behind schedule. It was eventually collected by Mr Cookson without ever being steamed or tested at Prospect Avenue, in fact the paint was still wet on the buffer planks as we loaded the engine on to Mr Cookson's trailer. The day after CORONATION left the workshops for Billingshurst, a telegram arrived from Mr Cookson to the effect that all the tests were perfectly satisfactory with the exception of a troublesome low-pressure injector. The locomotive, although carrying the name CORONATION on the splashers, was never fitted with number plates when it left Farnborough. It would have been numbered 4011 (fourth type, eleventh engine). Mr Cookson subsequently numbered it '2011', presumably because it was his second engine currently at Billingshurst.

The 'Fox Hill Miniature Railway' had now been changed to the 'Farnborough (Hants) Miniature Railway' for obvious reasons, as the line had developed into a public passenger-carrying railway as opposed to its original private concept.

In spite of the dubious circumstances concerning the cancellation of the 4-6-2 No.4010, Mr Kinloch did, however, place a firm order for an atlantic and work on this started in the summer of 1936. Captain Howey had also been in touch with my father and placed an order for a fifteen-inch gauge 4-6-2 based on the L.M.S.R. 'Princess' class. There was little or no week-day traffic on the railway as autumn approached. So only two engines needed to be steamed daily, usually WENDY and one of the tank engines. Maintenance and adjustment of the track was under the supervision of an ex-Southern Railway permanent way ganger. My duties included collecting the men and their equipment from the section of the track on which they had been working. One day, as I approached the curve through Lye Copse propelling two trucks with the pannier-tank engine No.3007 travelling chimney first, I had a distinctly uncomfortable feeling that the banking was much too severe. With the driver's seat positioned on the left side of the bunker, my weight had a further adverse effect on the engine. However, in the hands of such an experienced supervisor, I did not feel it was my place, as a junior driver, to criticise the work of a man of such high esteem.

Several of my father's friends and associates had visited the railway at weekends from time to time, Captain Holder had been along, Mr Burgoyne, Mr Cookson and Captain Howey had also spent a bit of time driving. On the Saturday following the week's maintenance, Mr Richardson, a rather portly gentleman, set off from Fox Hill on the pannier tank running light chimney-first to Hawley, with full tanks and plenty of coal in the bunker. After some twenty minutes or so one of the track maintenance men came hurrying up the line to report that the engine had "gorn over".

It seems the banking was indeed too severe round the curve and the weight of the driver had been just enough to tip the engine over; she fell down the bank and landed upside-down in the mud. Fortunately Mr Richardson had managed to get clear and was not injured. My father arrived from 'The Olives' and at first it was thought the engine would have to be dismantled where she lay, but Dad decided to try and get the one-ton Bedford recovery truck from Bradford's Garage reversed down the track and so winch the loco out. In fact this was achieved and within a week or two No.3007 was back in service none the worse for her exploits. The banking was considerably reduced after this incident, needless to say.

0-6-0T No. 3007 head on at Fox Hill. Note how the pannier tanks allow both the inside motion and the fittings on top of the boiler to remain accessible.

No. 2006 EDWARD VIII stands ready to depart tender-first from Hawley terminus, Fox Hill Miniature Railway. This was before the turning loop was laid.

A.D. Kinloch takes a well-loaded WESTERN QUEEN out of Fox Hill station, 1936.

4-6-2 No. 2573 HARVESTER raising steam outside the running shed at Foxhill.

CHAPTER VI — TRIUMPHS and DISASTERS

Evaluation trials and testing of the locomotives were always carried out during quiet periods, usually in the evenings. HARVESTER was lit up on one such evening about 4pm on a mid-week day, with the usual assistance from the stationary boiler. With pressure rising nicely in No.2573, my father took over the duties of attending to the engine, whilst my brother and I marshalled a very long test train made up of trucks, open and closed coaches, and the steel ballast wagon.

HARVESTER was by now blowing off like mad and with cylinder cocks open was taken gently forward over the turntable and out beyond the platforms to the signal gantry , where the points were set for her to be reversed on to her extraordinarily long train. After attending to the stationary boiler and topping up the water tower, using the last of the steam for the donkey pump, I climbed aboard the last coach and waved the green light for my father to proceed. After what was undoubtedly a fair degree of slipping, the 4-6-2 got hold of the heavy train and soon began to romp down the descent to Lye Copse, rounding the long curve. I now had my first clear view of the engine. With just a feather of steam from the safety valves drifting back towards the three saloon coaches in the middle of the train, HARVESTER looked really splendid in the setting sun with her apple green livery in shining contrast to the black smokebox and footplate.

We entered the copse over the first set of points at reduced speed and I offered the green light as soon as the wheels of the last coach were clear of the points, immediately receiving a 'toot' from the chime whistle accompanied by the sight of a shower of sparks from the chimney as my father opened his engine out. Accelerating through the last part of the woods, we emerged on to the flat approaches to the River Blackwater (shown as 'Cove Brook' on the map), and beyond beyond with a burst of speed to the 1 in 70 incline towards Hawley where the facing points controlling the loop were spring loaded in our favour. There was barely enough room to run round the train. The locomotive was then replenished with oil, water and coal, while my guard duties were handed over to my brother.

Taking advantage of the favourable road away from Hawley, HARVESTER fairly raced along the straight and over the river bridge with what I thought was a considerable amount of shouldering. Easing his engine down for entry into the darkening woods, we slowly negotiated the first set of points giving us the right hand road out from the loop. With the engine well clear of the second set of points my father opened the regulator for a good assault on the 1 in 74 bank. We had only travelled some 50-60yds however, when suddenly there was an almighty bang under the footplate of the engine and she began to lurch violently.

My father immediately brought the train to a halt. Examination revealed a bent pony truck axle, possibly caused by a 12lb per yd. section rail of the original track having been fishplated up to the newer 9lb per yd. material, leaving a pronounced flange. We uncoupled half the train and allowed the coaches to run down on to the loop where we derailed a few of the bogies to prevent a runaway. After the barrier was placed across the line my father began to ease HARVESTER gently up the gradient to the station approaches, where the shortened train was uncoupled. The engine was then reversed into the running shed where the fire was drawn and the boiler blown down.

The next day my brother and I decided to cycle over to the railway to fit the replacement axle ourselves. We detached the feed pipes to the injectors from the tender, uncoupled it and pushed it clear. Then with a car-type screw jack under each side of the engine below the cab, we wound the jacks up together until we had sufficient clearance, removing keeper plates from underneath the axleboxes without difficulty. We then offered up the replacement assembly by lying on the ground and locating the axlebox guides between the hornblocks. At that moment the jack on my side slipped and the engine fell back on to the track, trapping me by the arm. My brother Charles' first attempt to lift the rear of the engine with a crowbar only resulted in my arm being partly freed, but I was now pinned by my wrist and in great pain. My brother summoned help on the extension telephone to 'The Olives' and I can just about remember being dragged clear before passing out. I came round on my way to Dr. Bocket's Surgery, where it was discovered that my wrist was fractured. In spite of our good intentions we still got a good ticking off from Dad.

Bullock locomotives on a Bullock railway, at Farnborough in 1936. Left to Right: No. 2006 EDWARD VIII, driver H.C.S. Bullock; No. 2573 HARVESTER, driver 'Dumpy' Edenden (so called because he had lost part of a finger); 0-6-0PT No. 3007, driver K.A. Bullock; 0-4-2T No. 3008, driver K.A. Bullock; 0-4-2T No. 3008, driver Charles Bullock; 4-4-0 No. 2 WENDY; G.N.R. 4-2-2 No. 1

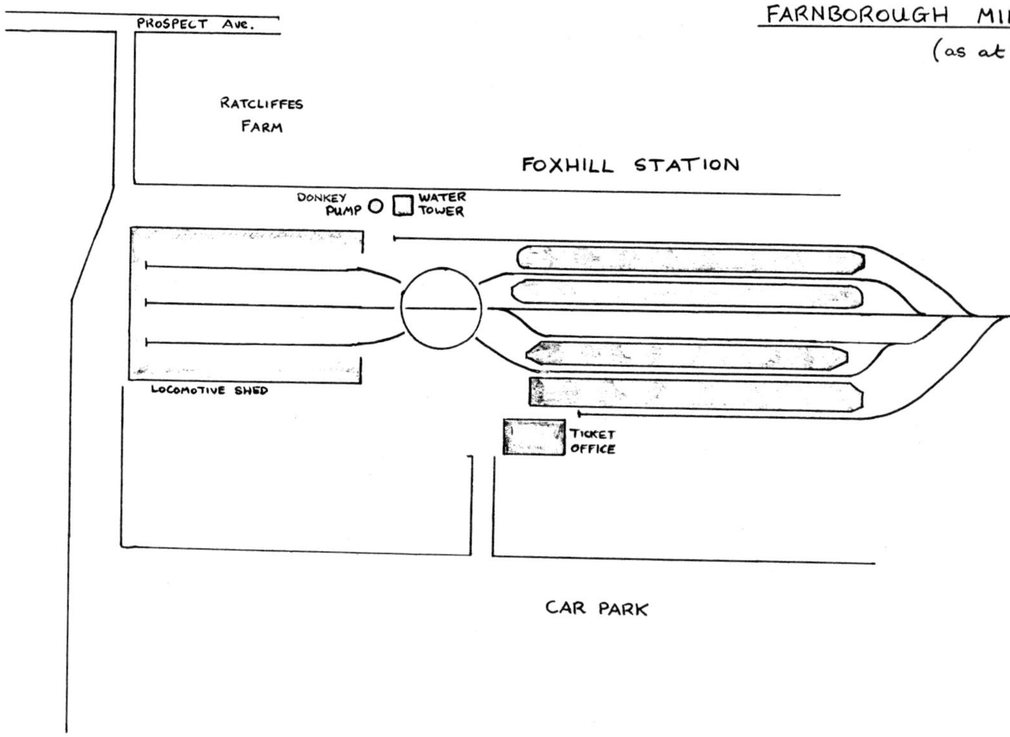

A 'one-off transaction' seen on open cars at Fox Hill in 1937-38. 'FCMR' stood for the then planned 'Frimley & Camberley Miniature Railway'. In fact the new line became the Surrey Border & Camberley Railway.

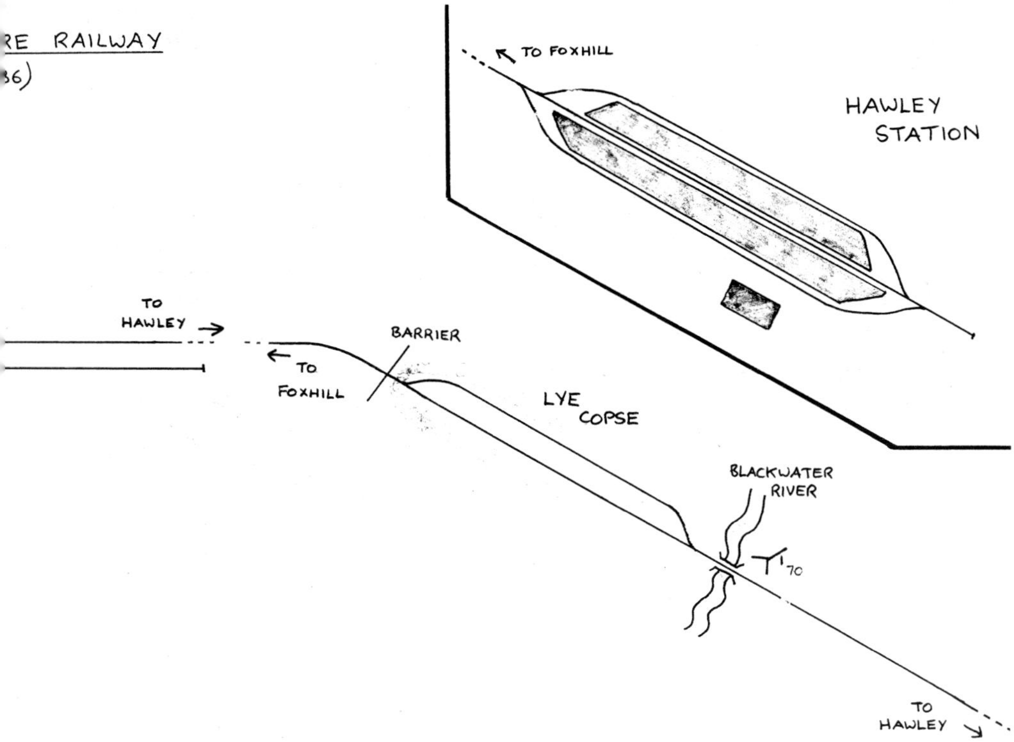

EDWARD VIII at Fox Hill station, Mr Cookson driving.

During the course of further trials, EDWARD VIII was tried fired on small coke. The steaming was not at all impaired, although there was a tendency to lift the fire when working hard. The locomotive proved capable of hauling 12 tons (over 150 passengers including the weight of the carriages) and was once timed to do 40mph on the road. A scale 1820 tons and a scale speed of 213mph !!

The Great Northern single-wheeler No.1 had been found quite unsuitable for hauling trains, as has been stated. It was therefore decided to mount the locomotive on to a flat one-ton platform lorry to advertise the F.M.R. With the driving axle raised clear of the rails and the locomotive running in steam, the lorry was parked outside such places as the Arcade Cinema in Camberley, the Ritz in Aldershot and other public places in the district.

4-4-2 No.4012 PRINCESS ELIZABETH was now completed and delivered late in the year to the railway. The engine was of similar specification to No.2005 but with cylinders of 5in. stroke and 3½ in. bore, slide valves and was finished in blue livery, by request from Mr Kinloch. The whistle was identical to No.2006 and it too was placed horizontally and had the same distinctive tone.

One weekday afternoon a few weeks after arrival at Fox Hill, PRINCESS ELIZABETH was pushed outside the engine house and made ready for steaming. A train of open coaches were assembled on one of the platform roads, whilst two hundredweight of dry sand was loaded on to a small four-wheel truck. With about 70lb per sq.in showing on the gauge of the 4-4-2, the three 4-6-2s Nos. 1003, 2006 and 2573 were hauled out from their respective roads in the engine shed and thoroughly oiled up, the reversing lever of each locomotive being set in the mid-gear position. The three dead engines coupled to the atlantic's tender were hauled forward to the end of the platform. They were then reversed on to the train of coaches (11 in all), the little sand truck being used meanwhile to sand about 50ft of track in front of PRINCESS ELIZABETH.

With my father at the controls and my brother and I in the sand truck coupled to the front of the engine, we set off gently from Fox Hill station over the slight inclined stretch beyond the signal gantry. Then came the easier length to the descent before the curve. In the sand truck we could feel the atlantic being hunted by the three free-running but heavy 4-6-2s as my father slowed his train for the loop points. Drawing to a halt the three dead engines eventually coupled to the train after much pushing and shoving. The sand truck had now to be propelled by No.4012 running tender first.

The purpose of this particular test, we were informed by my father, was to "ascertain the haulage capabilities of the 4-4-2 in relation to the locomotive's adhesive weight availability", which is why we began the test in the dark atmosphere of the woods, I suppose, instead of running through to Hawley. However, having applied sand to the wet rails well ahead of the engine, my father drew forward slowly until the train was out of the copse and the last coach clear, for the barrier to be replaced. Then, with only 30 yards or so of level road before the start of the incline, the atlantic was opened out in full backward gear and with some degree of controlled slipping she began to accelerate her heavy train.

4-6-2 No. 2011 CORONATION at Farnborough Green Station on the Surrey Border & Camberley Railway in 1939. Note temporary use of the six-wheel tender from 4-4-2 No. 4012.

No. 2006 EDWARD VIII passes under the noble signal gantry at the entrance to Fox Hill station.

From my crouched position in the truck I was enjoying the sound of the exhaust beat from the hard-working engine, when suddenly it changed to a roar which was accompanied by some mechanical noise from the left-hand side of the engine. After alighting from the tender my father examined the motion to find a broken expansion link. With the tools always carried on the tender, he removed the radius rod, combination lever and union link from the left-hand motion and, with baling twine acquired from the fence, secured the valve in mid-gear.

We uncoupled the coaches from the engine and pushed them gently down to the barrier. Not knowing quite what was going to happen my brother and I stood by as my father got back on to the engine, indicating that we should give the locomotives a push. Our efforts were rewarded with the first exhaust beat from the crippled locomotive as it strained to keep its heavy load moving up the incline on one cylinder. As the mist rolled down the meadow silhouetting the cattle against the darkening sky, I detected a wry smile as the glow from the fire-hole caught my father's warm features. As his engine was holding its own against the 1 in 74 gradient and the signal gantry was coming into view, we felt the worst was over. It was a relief to hear the weird exhaust from PRINCESS ELIZABETH diminish as she drifted down the platform with her precious load to the safety of the turntable and engine shed. After the locomotives had been put away, I remember my father driving us home in silence, although no doubt his mind was very actively engaged in some calculations pertaining to tractive effort.

CHAPTER VII — LAST STEAMINGS

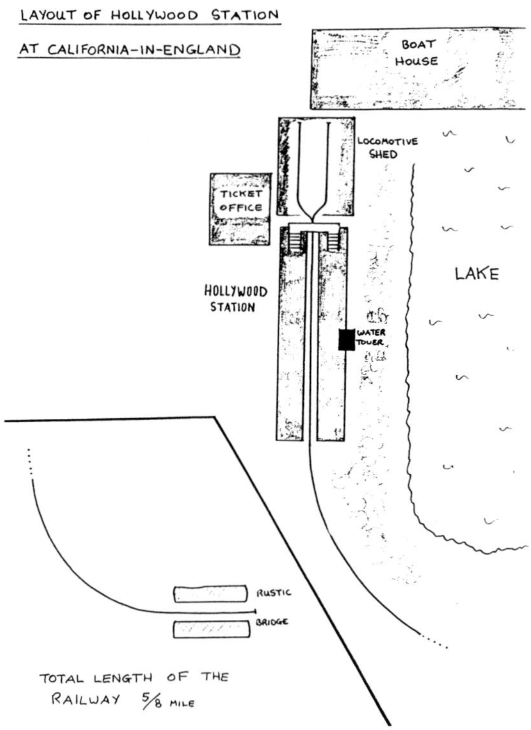

Mr Kinloch or Dr Bernard would sometimes telephone 'The Olives' requesting an engine to be made available on a Sunday when the line would normally be closed for the winter. On one such occasion Dr Bernard rang for HARVESTER to be in steam for his arrival at the line; the locomotive was made ready for mid-morning and driven to the end of the platform while steam was being raised in the 0-4-2T.

When Dr Bernard arrived he donned his overalls and set off down the line on HARVESTER running light. When we realised he had left the station we blew the whistle on No. 3008 but to no avail. We could only wait for the inevitable to occur — the barrier across the railway line separating the grazing land from the copse had not been removed!

It was always recognised as the one outstanding rule since the beginning of the railway that the first driver in the morning removed the barrier and the last driver at night replaced it. Of course Dr Bernard knew of this arrangement but it would not normally apply to him or Mr Kinloch as both these gentlemen usually arrived at and departed from the railway between these duties being performed.

Sure enough, it was not long before Dr Bernard was seen staggering up the track, his face covered with blood. HARVESTER had crashed through the bottom of the barrier breaking the lower of the two stout silver birch poles, the upper one dislodging the Doctor from the tender. HARVESTER's bogie became derailed by the collision. As I was the youngest member of the staff present I took the full force of Dr Bernard's wrath.

This incident, together with the ordering then cancelling of the 4-6-2 No.4010, together with other unsavoury aspects at the railway, tipped the scales. The result was that early in 1937 my father removed his two engines, some rolling stock and sufficient of his original 12lb per yd rail etc. as he would need for a line of his own.

He had come to an arrangement with the proprietor of the leisure complex called California-in-England, near Eversley, Hampshire, for building a line there. Work began immediately clearing ground and soon a single-line track was laid half way round the lake with the station ('Hollywood') and engine shed adjacent to the boat house, as shown on the plan opposite.

The length of the line was five-eighths of a mile and the layout the simplest possible but this leisure park which was so far in advance of its time was a delightful setting for a railway. The line wound its way round the pine and beech trees, through areas of cultivated rhododendrons offering glimpses of the water lilies and black swans on the lake. After one more easy curve the track straightened to its terminus beyond an old rustic bridge, a shown below with No. 3008 in action, my father driving. Passengers could alight after a single journey and return on a later train. Some Sundays we were so busy both engines were used double-headed to haul the fully loaded coaches. Mr Cookson was keen to buy the 0-4-2T No. 3008 and a 4-4-0 tender engine was hastily constructed to replace it. The new locomotive was No. 5013 and had outside cylinders with slide valves. It utilized the copper boiler removed from the old single-wheeler from Pitmaston Moor. The 4-4-0 had a six-wheel tender and, in keeping with the character of the line, a proper cow-catcher. The locomotive was painted in G.W.R. colours and had a copper-capped chimney and brass dome. The latter was partly filled with lead, which added quite a few pounds to assist adhesion. It is illustrated as it existed in later years bearing the number 3009, on pages 62-63.

In due course, the 0-4-2T No. 3008 was moved to Billingshurst as traffic began to fall off and in September it was replaced at California by the 4-4-0. In October the 0-6-0PT No. 3007 was returned to Prospect Avenue, the 4-4-0 remaining at California under lock and key.On 20 November 1937, my father, now physically and mentally exhausted, passed away peacefully at 'The Olives'. As he was laid to rest in the little cemetery behind the South Eastern & Chatham Railway's Reading-Tonbridge line, the through train from Birkenhead to Ramsgate hauled by a resplendent three cylinder 'mogul', drifted down towards North Farnborough Box urgently whistling up for the outer home. It seemed to be a tribute to my father's contribution to the world of miniature railways, a contribution which is not likely to be repeated by one man alone.

The little side tank 0-4-2T No. 3008 like its maker nears the end of the line at California-in-England, Eversley, Hants, 1937.

APPENDIX — SYNOPSIS OF THE LOCOMOTIVES

It should first be said that the locomotives whose histories are described in these notes are arranged in the order in which they were allocated numbers by their builder. Bullock had his own system of numbering in which the design was indicated by the first digit of the number, while the 'Works Number' of each successive locomotive was indicated by the last two digits of the number. The series runs from '01' to '13' with two exceptions, '09' and '10'. The '09' in fact existed but being a scale model of the L.N.E.R 4-6-2 HARVESTER, in service it took the prototype's number 2573. No.2573 is described out of order.

'10' was to have been 4-6-2 No.4010 PRINCESS MARGARET ROSE for the 15in. gauge Romney, Hythe & Dymchurch Railway. In the event the order was cancelled after much construction work had been done. The incomplete chassis of this locomotive together with ancillaries patterns and drawings were removed from the workshops at Prospect Avenue in December 1937, after Mr Bullock's death, before the executors had sealed the unoccupied premises.

As a reminder of happier days and telling us what miniature railways are all about we see (right) 4-6-4 No. 1001 BUBBLES coming through the woods on Dudley Alexander's Meadow End Railway near Brockenhurst, Hants, some time in the mid-1960s. Of the large Bullock locomotives it is specially satisfying to record that all except two — 0-6-0T No.3008 and atlantic No.4012 — are still in existence and moreover, in the hands of owners who appreciate them. The only sad thing is that none of the big 4-6-2s are currently being operated on public lines in Britain.

On the other hand, regarding the seven smaller engines, the location of only one is known to the contributors to this appendix. This is the 5in.gauge G.W.R. 4-2-2 BLACK PRINCE is on display in the Romney, Hythe & Dymchurch Railway's exhibition hall at New Romney, Kent.

Lastly, it must be said that the later history of the Bullock locomotives is very complex and has tended to defeat those who have tried to write about it. This account attempts to give the bare bones of a considerable saga and it is hoped that readers will regard these notes as an appetizer for a more definitive account which hopefully is to come. These notes owe much to help given by others, notably John Hall-Craggs, Matthew Kerr, James Nutty and Simon Townsend.

CONTENTS

THE LOCOMOTIVE, August 14, 1937

MINIATURE RAILWAY EQUIPMENT

LOCOMOTIVES, CARRIAGES, WAGONS, SIGNALS, PERMANENT WAY, ETC., ETC.

10¼" Gauge Steam Locomotive, Shoreham-on-Sea Railway.

Practical experience in design and manufacture of locomotives for miniature passenger carrying railways.
Latest machinery for turning out well finished work.

Enquiries invited. Expert Advice and Estimates willingly given.

DESIGNER AND BUILDER OF THE MOST POWERFUL 10¼" GAUGE LOCOMOTIVE IN THE COUNTRY.

H. C. S. BULLOCK, PROSPECT AVE., FARNBOROUGH, HANTS.

In the May 1934 issue of 'THE LOCOMOTIVE RAILWAY CARRIAGE & WAGON REVIEW' H.C.S.Bullock described the details of his engineering practice ...

Miniature Pacific Type Locomotive
by H.C.S.Bullock

The engine illustrated below was built for the 10¼in. gauge by the writer to his own designs to produce a machine of maximum haulage power and at the same time to obtain accessibility to all working parts.

The two cylinders are 3½in. bore by 5 in. stroke, fitted with piston valves of 1 5/8 in. dia. and 1¼ in. travel. The valve timing provides for a steam lead of 1/64 in. and 75% cut-off in full gear. There is 1/64 in. exhaust clearance or negative lap. The valves are actuated by a modified Baker gear. The cylinders are lubricated by a mechanical lubricator with separate pump for each cylinder. Drain cocks are operated from the cab. Water pressure relief valves are fitted to the cylinder covers. Inspection covers are provided opposite the four ports so that the valves can be set by sight instead of the usual measuring on the valve spindle.

The driving and coupled wheels, 12in. in diameter, are heavy and wide on the treads, whilst the gauge is decreased slightly to enable the engine to run freely around curves of small radius, 35ft being negotiated with ease. The bogie wheels are 7in. diameter with the inside-framed bogie being allowed 1½in. lateral play. The rear truck is fitted with outside frames to clear the ashpan, which is sloped forward to allow the ash to drop on to the track; a front damper only is fitted. The pivot of the rear truck is in front and below the firebox. The wheels are 6in. diameter and the axle, which at times is heavily loaded, runs on ball bearings. A powerful steam brake is fitted and all brake blocks are compensated.

The boiler, which is after the pattern of that of the G.W.R 4-6-2 THE GREAT BEAR, is 13½ in. diameter at the front end and at the firebox end, 14½ in. The barrel is 4ft. long and the firebox outside is 2ft. long. Twenty-eight tubes 7/8in. dia. and eight flues 1 1/8in. dia. are provided. The grate area is 262sq.in and the heating surface 37sq.ft.

The combined safety valve and top feed is designed in the form of a small dome from which steam is collected. This dome is detachable and provides the inspection cover required by the Insurance companies.

The boiler is fed by one injector when standing and by a double-acting pump driven by the crosshead when running. A by-pass control valve is fitted and can be operated from the footplate.

The locomotive is 10ft. long, 21in. wide over the footplate and 30in high over the top of the cab.

The tender runs on two four-wheel bogies fitted with ball bearings, carries 28 gallons of water and provides ample seating accommodation for the driver. Its length is 5ft. 4in., making a total length over buffers of 15ft. 9in. The locomotive is so designed as to be easily converted to the 9½in. gauge.

Bullock says little about performance in this account, but one reads with awe of an hauling capacity of 12 tons (i.e. a train with 150 passengers) and of 40mph running — a scale 200mph! No doubt the wide-tread and deep-flanged wheels (above left) used by Bullock made these astronomical speeds safe, but equally remarkable is the ability of these 10¼ in. gauge locomotives to go round curves as sharp as 35ft radius.

George Woodcock in his book 'MINIATURE LOCOMOTIVES' speaks in glowing terms of such Bullock features as the easily get-at-able external regulator (see cab view above, right) as well as the simple lubricator drive which substitutes a simple contact arrangement for the usual ratchet-and-pawl. Woodcock also mentions that Bullock did not use superheaters, but this is incorrect as regards the later engines, which had a five-element one, as illustrated below. Woodcock rebuilt WESTERN QUEEN himself, so one assumes No.1003 was not so equipped. But a typical Bullock conundrum is the fact that his account opposite describes a boiler with superheater FLUES but makes no mention of a superheater!

After experience had been gained, some modifications were found to be necessary. Slide valves were substituted for piston valves and a second injector for the feed-pump. The first four locomotives (the 'Type 1's') originally had what Bullock described as 'modified Baker valve gear' instead of the more conventional Walschaerts. Baker gear was an American invention which even today has yet to be tried on a full-size locomotive in Britain, but its adoption was in the 1930s strongly advocated for little locomotives, by the legendary 'L.B.S.C.' in MODEL ENGINEER magazine. Its advantage lies in the fact that there are no difficult-to-machine curved slides, only plain pins and bushes. However, in this case there seems to have been a problem and conventional Walschaerts gear was soon substituted as well as being fitted to subsequent engines. Another modification beginning with No.1004 was the use of single-bar crossheads for the cylinders. In Bullock's day neither this feature nor the use of outside valve gear were normal Great Western practice, but he was strangely prophetic because the last Swindon design — the neat 0-6-0Ts of the 15XX class — had both these features.

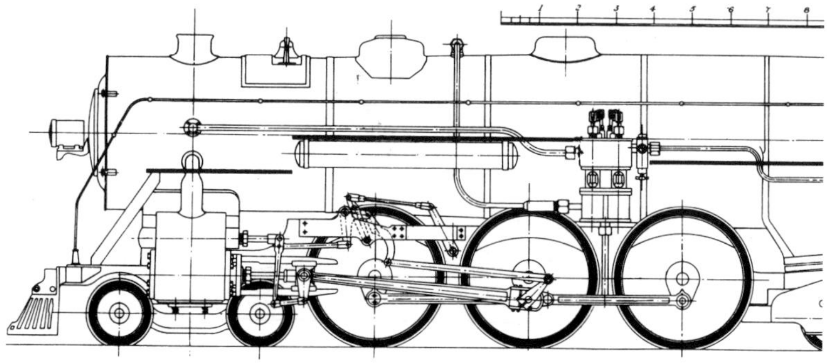

Drawing of Baker Valve Gear

Baker Valve Gear on No. 1003 WESTERN QUEEN

Single-bar crosshead and Walschaerts motion on No. 2005 PRINCESS MARINA

NON-BULLOCK LOCOMOTIVES

The later history of the Bullock locomotive is complicated by the fact that Bullock designs and, in some cases, parts were incorporated in locomotives built by others. John Thurston had worked for Bullock and after his death produced no less than seven 4-6-2s and 4-6-4s. One of these (illustrated above ready for action at Reading, Berks) confusingly bore the nameplates WESTERN QUEEN. The best-known 'Thurstons' were 12¼ in. gauge 4-6-4s with Bullock features and possibly a few Bullock parts — which long worked the miniature railway at Littlehampton, Sussex, as shown below. Another maker of Bullock look-alikes was the Motor Gear & Engineering Co. which in 1947 built two 4-6-2s PRINCE and PRINCESS, the latter now operating at Bressingham Hall, Diss, Norfolk.

4-6-2 No. 1001 THE MONARCH
(later AUDREY then BUBBLES)

4-6-2 No.1001 THE MONARCH (soon to be AUDREY) was completed in 1932 for Captain Holder of 'Keeping', Beaulieu, Hants, as seen above receiving an editorial visit from the MODEL ENGINEER, about 1935. Left to right are Messrs Maskelyne, Captain Holder, his son Terry and Mr.Hill, Holder's chauffeur-mechanic. Incidentally, there was a clock over the portico with the legend 'Keeping Time'. Bullock made the boiler for this engine but with limited facilities at Fowler Road at this time, it was not a very satisfactory job. A new boiler by Goodhand was fitted in 1936, seen being offered up below. At some time also the Baker valve gear was replaced by Walschaerts, a sand-dome added and, much later, the rear pony truck replaced by a bogie, making the locomotive a 4-6-4. All this work was carried out at Beaulieu.

During the war No.1001, now named AUDREY, was loaned to the War Department to demonstrate to Commando troops the most effective use of explosives for destroying enemy locomotives. In 1952 No.1001 was bought by Dudley Alexander of Brockenhurst and ran during the summer months on his circular layout at Meadow End. Here the locomotive, now named BUBBLES after one of her owner's favourite ponies, ran 1300 miles earning some £2,000 for charities, as seen above with the author in the driving seat. Note that the sand-dome is not mounted.

In 1964 BUBBLES was acquired by John Fowles, moved to his Stonecot Hill Railway at Carshalton, Surrey and given an overhaul, as seen below now with the sand-dome replaced. The engine was subsequently moved to Hayling Island and is now privately owned near Guildford, Surrey, but is currently in process of changing hands.

4-6-2 No. 1002 THE EMPRESS

4-6-2 No.1002 THE EMPRESS was built in 1933 for Mr Cookson of Billingshurst, Sussex. After two seasons the engine was returned to Farnborough for re-gauging for Mr Burgoyne's successive 9½ in. gauge lines at Crowthorne Farm and Spring Lanes (where she is seen above with Mr Maskelyne driving) near Bracknell. Burgoyne later 'South-Africanised' the engine by fitting a foreign type of cab and American tender. He removed the nameplates, mounting one rather strangely in front of the chimney. The locomotive was painted yellow. In this state No.1002 is depicted below when, after Burgoyne's death, she was bought by Ron Hammett of Bexleyheath, Kent, and run in Danson Park there.

After several seasons running in Danson Park THE EMPRESS (now with her nameplates in the correct place, as seen above) was sold to a small company called 'M.E. Locomotives' and run for three seasons in a park in Hornchurch, Essex. The company disbanded and Hammett bought the locomotive back again but later sold her to Barking Council. As is shown below the 'British' appearance was happily restored, in the course of a major overhaul. No.1002 operated in Barking Park until 1962, when it was sold to an operator who brought the engine down to Ferndown, Dorset. THE EMPRESS is now undergoing a major overhaul near Bath.

4-6-2 No. 1003 WESTERN QUEEN

4-6-2 No.1003 WESTERN QUEEN was built in 1934 and went to a Mr Ballance who used her on his public line at Burnham-on-Sea, Somerset, (as shown above) for one season. She was returned to Farnborough for repairs, then operated during the construction of the line at Fox Hill. The locomotive was later transferred to the Surrey Border & Camberley Railway until that line closed in 1940. Charles Lane then bought the engine and ran it on his short line at Liphook, Hants — 'The Royal Anchor Miniature Railway'. It was sold by Lane and later operated at Lowestoft, Suffolk, and Plymouth (see below) and Paignton in Devon. At Paignton children put sand down the chimney and damaged the cylinders.

No.1003 then passed through the hands of George Woodcock, who replaced the damaged piston-valve cylinders by slide-valve ones, before disposing of the engine to Maurice Densham's line at North Tawton, Devon. As may be seen above, she still maintains her dignity in spite of indifferent treatment afforded her by a succession of different owners. The locomotive is now privately owned and operable near St.Austell, Cornwall, as seen below 'on shed'. During the time that No.1003 was at Plymouth in 1948, a 10¼in. gauge steam locomotive which carried very distinctive Bullock hall-marks to the front end and motion was in operation there. This engine was completed by John Thurston of Prospect Road, Farnborough.

4-6-4 No. 1004 MARY

4-6-4T No.1004 MARY — not the most attractive-looking of the Bullock locomotives — was built for Captain Holder of 'Keeping', Beaulieu, Hants, where she ran with the two atlantics PETER PAN and JOHN TERENCE and the Bullock pacific No.1001. The 4-6-4, by then converted from a tank to a tender engine, was sold after Captain Holder's death. Later the smokebox and truncated chassis were butchered to form a crude steam-outline i.c.-engined 4-4-0 for a line at Morecambe, Lancs. Recently the remains came into the possession of Jeff Price of Watford.

4-6-2 No. 2573 HARVESTER

4-6-2 No.2573 HARVESTER was built in 1936 for the Fox Hill Miniature Railway, as shown above. She was notionally transferred to the Surrey Border & Camberley Railway in 1938 but there is no evidence of her having worked there. As seen below, a few years afterwards No.2573 was shipped to India, having been bought by the Gaekwar of Baroda (Vadodra) to run in his palace gardens, now a public park. Note a genuine FHMR Pullman car.

4-6-2 No. 2005 SILVER JUBILEE
(briefly PRINCESS MARINA finally KING GEORGE VI)

4-6-2 No.2005 SILVER JUBILEE was completed in 1935, as shown above outside the workshop at Prospect Avenue. She was built for Mr Cookson of Billingshurst, Sussex and ran on his private railway. She was also operated on lines at Shoreham-by-Sea and in the grounds of Bramber Castle, as seen below. No.2005 went in 1938 to the Surrey Border & Camberley Railway and ran there until that line closed in 1939.

Later No.2005 ran for a few years on Kerr's Miniature Railway at Arbroath, Scotland, as seen above wearing 'Express Passenger Train' headcode. The engine was then bought by a garage proprietor in the Midlands. Later she was discovered in a semi-derelict state and brought down to the Stonecot Hill Railway at Carshalton, Surrey, as illustrated on the cover. Here a complete overhaul was undertaken. After spending a few years on Hayling Island, No.2005, now privately owned and named KING GEORGE VI, went back to mainland Sussex, as seen below on exhibition at Midhurst in 1980.

4-6-2 No. 2006 EDWARD VIII (later PRINCESS ELIZABETH)

Those numerous enthusiasts who considered the Great Western Railway as towering over its contemporaries had plenty of excuses as to why the GWR failed to build a class of modern 4-6-2s. But only one of them actually did something about it and that was H.C.S. Bullock. How well he succeeded is particularly well demonstrated in the illustrations here reproduced of 4-6-2 No.2006 EDWARD VIII, completed in the winter of 1935-36. No.2006 followed WESTERN QUEEN to Fox Hill, where we see (above) No.2006 at Hawley station. Bullock is known to have regarded No.2006 as his favourite amongst all his creations and frequently drove this much admired locomotive.

In 1938 No.2006 was transferred to the Surrey Border & Camberley Railway, receiving the six-wheel tender from the ill-fated atlantic PRINCESS ELIZABETH. The engine is seen (centre) on the Camberley turntable and again (below) at the unfinished Camberley station, having in the meantime been fitted with a longer chimney.

After the S.B.C.R. closed No.2006 was abandoned for two years, surrounded by tomato plants in the boarded-up Farnborough Green station. No.2006 later went to Stourport, Worcestershire, then to Maurice Denham's line at North Tawton, Devon. No.2006 now has the nameplates from PRINCESS ELIZABETH and is privately owned near St. Austell, Cornwall, as illustrated (above) ready for action with Matthew Kerr, proprietor of Kerr's Miniature Railway, Arbroath, Scotland, at the helm and (below) 'on shed'.

0-6-0T No. 3007
(later 0-6-0 FIREFLY)

0-6-0 pannier tank No.3007 was built in 1936 for the Fox Hill Miniature Railway where, in company with 0-4-2T side-tank No.3008, it can be seen above. No.3007 was used to open Bullock's line at California-in-England, near Eversley, Hants, in the spring of 1937. In October the locomotive was returned to Farnborough where it remained until December, when it was moved to Dymchurch, Kent. Rebuilt to a tender engine and re-named FIREFLY, No.3007 worked on the line at 'Rock-a-Nore', Hastings, Sussex, as seen opposite. No.3007 is now owned by Matthew Kerr and runs on his famous railway at Arbroath, Scotland (below).

0-4-2T (later 0-6-0T) No. 3008

0-4-2T side-tank No.3008 was completed shortly after No.3007 for the Fox Hill Miniature Railway, later accompanying the pannier tank to California-in-England near Eversley, Hants. Mr Cookson bought the locomotive towards the end of the running season and operated it at Shoreham-by-Sea as seen above. It was then transferred to the Surrey Border & Camberley Railway where, as shown below, it was rebuilt as an 0-6-0T. After that No.3008 worked on a line at Severn Beach, near Bristol, followed by a rumour of shipment from Avonmouth Docks to India. No. 3008 is the only one of the larger Bullock locomotives to be lost without trace; nothing is known of the little engine's fate.

4-6-2 No. 2011 CORONATION (later MIGHTY ATOM)

4-6-2 No.2011 CORONATION was completed late in 1936 for Mr Cookson of Billinghurst, Sussex, and moved to the Surrey Border & Camberley Railway in 1938, as seen above. After the SB&CR closed No.2001 spent a short time with Mr Burgoyne of Crowthorne; it was then acquired by Albert Reeve, re-named MIGHTY ATOM and run on his line at Perry Hall near Birmingham, as shown below. Mr Reeve had to sell up in 1955 and No.2011, by now rather dilapidated, was bought by T.F.Cooke of Wootton Wawen, a timber merchant. She is now in store 'somewhere in Mid-Wales'.

4-4-2 No. 4012 PRINCESS ELIZABETH

4-4-2 No.4012 PRINCESS ELIZABETH was Bullock's only 'atlantic'. She was built in 1936 for the Fox Hill Miniature Railway, as depicted below. Apart from the wheel arrangement, she was generally similar to the later 4-6-2s, except for the shorter boiler and smaller six-wheel tender. It was apparently intended to use her on the Surrey Border & Cambrerley Railway and, as shown above opposite, she was painted blue and lettered S.B.C.R. However, before the SB&CR opened, the engine seems to have met with a serious accident. This occurred in late 1937 or early 1938 because in the first half of 1938 No.4012 was loaded on to a Bedford lorry together with No.2573 HARVESTER, the accident-damaged 4-4-0 WENDY and the bogie tender body from No.2006 EDWARD VIII. They all went to Kitson's Works in Leeds, driven by 'Dumpy' Edenden and accompanied by Ron Brown, a junior driver on the SB&CR, then under construction.

In due course both HARVESTER and WENDY came back, but the boiler and other usable parts of the 4-4-2 No.4012 — as well as its number but not its name — plus the tender tank from No.2006 were incorporated into an articulated 2-6-0 + 0-6-2 Beyer-Garratt type locomotive, the first of two. The six-wheel tender belonging to PRINCESS ELIZABETH was then attached to EDWARD VIII.

The new No.4012 went into service (see lower illustration, opposite) on the SB&CR but was not wholly satisfactory. The small carrying wheels at each end were not mounted in pony trucks but ran in axleboxes in the main frames, making the engine less flexible than it might have been. Moreover the boiler would have been a trifle small to supply four cylinders. Years later this Garratt came, via Charles Lane of Liphook, into the hands of Sir Thomas Salt of Shillingstone, Dorset, who had the engine given a 'narrow-gauge' look. No.4012 has recently been sold but remains in private hands. Incidentally, the tale that the second Kitson Garratt went to India is incorrect, as it is at present in Norfolk.

S.B.&C.R
4012

4-4-0 No. 5013
(later GLADSTONE then IVANHOE)

4-4-0 No.5013 was built in 1937 for service on a railway at California-in-England near Eversley, Hants, by H.C.S.Bullock. He is seen (above left) at Prospect Avenue occupied in testing and freeing up the motion.

The basis of the locomotive was a second-hand boiler recovered from an early and discarded single-driver locomotive, originally used on Captain Holder's Pitmaston Moor Railway. No.5013 was intended to replace the 0-4-2T No.3008, which had gone to Mr Cookson for use at Shoreham-by-Sea. The engine subsequently passed through Thurston's hands after Bullock's death.

Later No.5013 — some accounts refer to her as No.3009 — went to Kerr's Miniature Railway, Arbroath, Scotland, as depicted here in four views. Note the bicycle lights used as headlamps. In Scotland No.5013 was called GLADSTONE, but it was more a nick-name than a proper name since nameplates were never fitted. In 1953 she was with Charles Lane of the Royal Anchor Hotel, Liphook. Then 5013 went to George Woodcock and after that was sold to a Mr Peter Hanton from Glossop, Cheshire. Recently, over quite a period of years the little 4-4-0 has been receiving a thorough overhaul which has included a new boiler. Finally in August 1987 the locomotive, now named IVANHOE, once again entered public service on Peter Hanton's Rudyard Lake Railway, Rudyard, Staffs.

SURREY BORDER & CAMBERLEY RAILWAY

In this book there are many references to the Surrey Border & Camberley Railway (S.B.C.R.). H.C.S.Bullock had little to do with it but early in 1938 after his death the Fox Hill — later the Farnborough (Hants) — Miniature Railway (F.H.M.R) was superseded by the S.B.C.R., which was directly descendant from the F.H.M.R. The S.B.C.R. was a grandiose concept which was cut off on the brink of success by the outbreak of war. The principal station Farnborough Green (seen above with No.2005, driven by Doctor Bernard, leaving and No.2006 awaiting departure on the right) was located at Fimley Bridges in Surrey, now the site of British Car Auctions. The line ran parallel to the old South Eastern & Chatham Railway's Reading-Tonbridge line for a quarter of a mile, then curved away to cross the Blackwater River, terminating after a run of about two miles in Camberley near the Blackwater Gas Works. Many of Bullock's locomotives worked on the S.B.C.R..

The railway was officially opened on 23rd July 1938 by Graham Moffat (one of the stars of the film 'Oh! Mr Porter') driving No.2011 CORONATION. The line closed on the outbreak of war, never to reopen. We see below No.2006 'in the hole' at Watchetts Wood station en route to Farnborough Green.